Imitation of Life

Books by Allison Joseph

What Keeps Us Here
Soul Train
In Every Seam
Imitation of Life

Imitation of Life

Poems by Allison Joseph

Carnegie Mellon University Press
Pittsburgh 2003

Acknowledgments

The author and publisher gratefully acknowledge editors of the
following journals in which these poems first appeared:

"La Marqueta," "Questions About Toys"—*Salamander*
"The Black Santa, "On Being Told I Don't Speak Like a Black
Person"—*Many Mountains Moving*
"Appetites," "Bullies," "Sleepaway Camp"—*Footwork: The Paterson
Literary Review*
"Mrs. Gaither"—*Acorn Whistle*
"Music Appreciation," "Shake Your Body"—*Karamu*
"Supermercado"—*Calliope*
"Salt"—*New Delta Review*
"Incommunicado"—*Half Tones to Jubilee*
"Father Meets Satchmo in Heaven"—*Charlotte Poetry Review*
"Frying Hair"—*Earth's Daughters*
"Double Dutch"—*Tamaqua*
"Explaining Sex to the Seventh Grade"—*Nerve Cowboy*
"Anti-Prom"—*Lone Wolf Review*
"Numbers"—*Prairie Schooner*
"Cammie Cuts My Hair"—*Musing Magazine*
"Searching for *Melinda's Magic Moment*—*Spoon River Poetry Review*
"Translating My Parents"—*Spindrift*
"The Principal"—*Pink Cadillac*

Book Design: Cassandra Knight

Publication of this book is supported by a grant from
the Pennsylvania Council on the Arts.

Library of Congress Control Number 2002101895
ISBN 0-88748-386-0 Pbk.

10 9 8 7 6 5 4 3 2 1

Contents

III

This book is dedicated to the memory of my father,
Everest Joseph.

I

La Marqueta

Remember the market beneath the el,
the wooden stalls that shook each time
a train rumbled overhead? Such plenty
in one place—dozens and dozens
of narrow booths jammed together,

sawdust strewn all over the dirty
floors, old women, scarf-wrapped,
arms loaded with bags of bargains,
shrieking at the butchers in shrill Spanish
or bitter English, taunting those men

in their bloodied white coats,
watching, sharp-eyed, for fingers
on the scales. Young, fascinated,
I watched them too—loud, proud men
working their stalls, whistling aloud,

hoisting sharpened cleavers and knives
to strip and slice and hack
at massive slabs of beef or pork,
paring away fat, bone, gristle.
They'd claim to pick the best fish

especially for you—top trout or red snapper,
pinkest salmon, greatest calamari and shrimp
this side of Italy laid out on wide beds
of crushed and shattered ice.
My family came on weekends

to buy what we couldn't find
elsewhere—fleshy round breadfruit
big as cannonballs, mounds
of succulent mangoes ripening,
each one full of juicy yellow pulp,

bulla cake—high, dense, brown,
a Caribbean cross between a cookie
and a biscuit, moist and sweet
from dark brown sugar.
We admired hefty wedges

of provolone or Gouda,
picked weighty yams,
gnarled ginger roots thick
as twisted fingers, bought sacks
of huge green callaloo leaves,

of dried codfish coated white with salt.
La Marqueta was better than any
carnival or circus, more real—
piñatas swinging from the rafters
of one booth, fried fish sizzling

in another, long lovely bananas here
larger than anywhere in the city,
unblemished in smooth yellow skins,
cool to my wandering fingers,
firm to my faithful touch.

Searching for *Melinda's Magic Moment*

I wonder if I could find it,
beloved book of my childhood
whose story transported me
past ordinary black girl status
to the rarefied life of Melinda,
a brown-skinned charmer who longed

to sing and dance on-stage
so everyone could roar their applause,
captivated by her dazzling talent.
I remember its coarse cover
of woven green cloth, its large type,
pages soiled by fingers of girls

who took it from the library
to read it in their rooms,
dreaming of being as pretty
as Melinda, as adored by adults.
Every teacher loved her—
her cute nose that wasn't

too broad, her lips that weren't
too full, her head of Shirley
Temple curls. But beauty
wasn't enough for Melinda,
who wanted nothing but to be
the lead in the school play,

a production of *Alice in Wonderland*
that called for a petite blonde Alice
used to pinafores, bows, white stockings.
So desperate was Melinda that she
powdered her brown skin pale,
perched a wig of fat yellow curls

on her head, put on her best dress—
one her momma kept pressed
for Easter—and she auditioned
for the role, won it, loved
all the more for her sweet

singing voice, her poise
under piled-on make-up.
She was the girl everyone cheered,
the gifted child we all hoped to be
before mirrors and magazines
told us otherwise.
So if you find this book

at some swap meet or garage sale,
if you dig it out of your mom's attic
or grandmother's basement, send it to me.
I'd like to read it again, touch it, see
if it's like I remember. And then,
I'd like to burn it.

The Black Santa

I remember sitting on his bony lap,
fake beard slumping off his face,
his breath reeking sweetly of alcohol,
a scent I didn't yet know at five.
And I didn't know that Santa
was supposed to be fat, white, merry—
not shaky and thin like this
department store Santa who listened
as I reeled off that year's list:
a child's oven I'd burn my fingers on,
a mini record player of gaudy plastic
I'd drag from room to room
by its precarious orange handle,
an Etch-a-Sketch I'd ruin by twisting
its dials too hard—my requests
as solemn as prayer, fervid, fueled
by too many hours of television,
too many commercials filled
with noisy children elated
by the latest game or toy.
I bet none of them
ever sat on the lap of a Santa
who didn't ho-ho-ho in jolly mirth,
whose sunken red eyes peered
out from under his oversized wig
and red velveteen cap, his teeth yellow,
long fingers tinged with yellow.

I did not find it strange
to call this man Santa,
to whisper my childish whispers
into his ear, to pull on his sleeve
to let him know I really deserved
all that I'd asked for. I posed
for an instant photo with him,
a woolen cap over my crooked braids,
mittens sewn to my coat sleeves.
No one could have convinced me
this Santa couldn't slide down
any chimney, though his belly
didn't fill his suit, and his hands
trembled, just a bit, as he lifted
me from his lap. No one could
have told me that a pink-cheeked
pale-skinned Santa was the only Santa
to worship, to beg for toys and candy.
I wouldn't have believed them,
wouldn't have believed anyone
who'd tell me Santa couldn't look
like me: brown eyes, face, skin.

Questions About Toys

Growing up, did you ever think
that boys owned better toys
than girls—did you ever want
to ditch your 11-inch fashion doll
for a rip-snorting, grenade-toting

G.I. Joe, that valiant muscled hero
who drove a rugged desert jeep
the same surly green as his army fatigues?
Did you ever want to pull back
on accurate, dangerous slingshots,

seeing how far you could launch a rock,
to palm a b.b. gun, spraying pellets
everywhere, or fondle a Swiss Army knife,
one with real blades, a fork, a screwdriver?
Given a choice, would you have traded away

those squalling dolls that sucked
on bogus baby bottles only to wet
themselves, diapers damp, clingy,
cold to the touch, would you
have turned from your charming

tea set with its miniature faux china
cups, its innocuous plastic spoons and plates
decorated with placid lilies, goldenrod?
Perhaps you had a toy kitchen, complete
with sink, ironing board, washer and dryer,

while your younger brother or first cousin
or the snotty-nosed little boy next door
spent all day lining up one-inch soldiers
in his backyard's immense grasses,
his green men frozen to their weapons,

their bayonets, rifles, muskets?
Would you have given up all those
precisely detailed doll clothes—
pink gingham dresses, gold evening
gowns, ruffled party outfits

with lace sleeves, fake fur muffs?
What would you have given for one
session of play that wasn't dainty
or circumspect, one hour when you didn't
need to care about keeping your doll's

limbs clean, intact, one afternoon when
you didn't pretend to clean and cook like
Mommy did, one moment when you reared back
and threw whatever was handy—rocks, sticks,
clods of dirt—imagining yourself invincible,

believing your strength superhuman,
your aim flawless, your arm
propelling that bit of the world
forward, forward, over the highest
fence, the furthest gate?

Translating My Parents

When my father would growl,
wash the wares now, I always thought
he'd said w-e-d-s, learned to move
to the sink quickly, in terror,

knew his order meant
wash the dishes right away,
and don't use too much soap.
And when Mother asked me

to put *serviettes* on the table,
I knew she meant *set the table,*
use napkins, the paper kind.
What sort of English was this

that they spoke so surely,
an odd lingo of strange terms
like *brolly* and *dustbin*
for umbrella and trashcan,

flannel instead of washcloth,
plimsolls instead of sneakers?
Baffled by their love
of fish and chips, crisps

and crumpets, I wondered
why they drank tea instead of coffee,
why my father downed Guinness
instead of Miller High Life,

making me sip that dark bitter stout,
laughing as I grimaced, wrinkling
my eight-year-old nose. I couldn't
imagine them living in any other

country but this one, in any other
house but this one, couldn't imagine
the house of my birth—289 Wightman Road,
London borough of Haringey.

The only borough I knew was the Bronx,
and there an elevator was an elevator,
not a *lift*, a cookie was a cookie,
not a *biscuit*, and no one dared call

sausage and potatoes *bangers and mash*.
I learned to translate their dialect
into an English I could recognize,
so when my father nagged

write a zed, and write it properly,
I knew he truly meant *write a Z,*
as in zipper, as in zero, and write
it plainly, so I can read it.

Double Dutch

If I raised my body just right,
no rope would crack my thin
brown ankles, my feet

thudding pavement instead,
landing safely between
two quickly turning ropes.

If I timed my move right,
I could spin within those
twirling lengths, execute

a 360° while still keeping
my balance, not stopping
the ropes' constant motion,

not interrupting the girls
whose outstretched arms
moved faster and faster,

until I lost my breath,
unable to lift my feet
any longer. Little else

to do in our neighborhood
of white-collar aspirations
and working-class jobs,

so we resourceful daughters
staged intricate championships
in the street, double dutch

played after school, on
weekends, all day long in
summer. Swaying to the

ever-shifting rhythms
of the ropes, we chanted
aloud to keep score,

sped it up if any
girl stayed in too long,
defying street wisdom

to dazzle us all, legs
pumping, feet quickening
as she kept moving,

outlasting us all in
a game we played
so fiercely our bodies

grew sore, muscles
aching from the jumping
and turning, the

tricky motions
of instinct and skill,
split-second timing

honed in driveways,
backyards, on sidewalks
and out in the streets

where cars would honk
us out of their way,
stopping play for just

one minute, one moment,
bodies poised to begin again
soon as each car sailed by,

kicking up dust in its wake,
but not dissuading us
from where we needed to be.

Frying Hair

Kitchen tile grainy beneath bare feet,
I crouch and perch on a shaky chair,
worn towel slung across my shoulders,
head thrust forward as Mother pulls

the burning metal comb through my
stiff woolen hair, snags buried deep
in the just-washed mass of tangles.
Teeth clenched against the tugging,

I try to hold my head still,
neck cramping as Mother works
inch-by-inch, section-by-section,
thick grease melting, liquefying,

helping the slick hot comb creep
though the knots, the tears,
as my hair comes out in tufts
I hold in one tense fist.

I want to ask my mother
what's so great about straight hair,
and why the woman on the jar
of Dax pressing grease looks

like a white woman, a lady
who'd never end up with burn marks
on ears or neck or forehead.
I want to ask why she

and every other black mother I know
insists on filling their homes
with this peculiar scent, this aroma
of mangled and burnt hair.

But she'd only call me rude, ungrateful,
tell me to hold still for fear the comb would
slip from her grasp, the fiery tool's teeth
dangerous if she made one tiny error,

if she set the comb on the burner
too long, blue gas flame searing it
into beauty's harshest weapon.
And after Mother transforms

my coarse kinks to shiny strands,
then come the tight braids
or the rollers, or the curling iron,
scalp more sore from the cute hairstyle

forced on my head. Was it cruelty?
Was it love—this skill passed on
from mother to obedient daughter?
My father would laugh out loud

at the scene in his kitchen, teasing
about *fried hair*, having never suffered
beneath the comb, never squirmed
or flinched in fear of damaging heat.

The Principal

When he walked the halls
of P.S. 38, his heavy steps
echoing off tile, frame clad

in dark, severe suits
that hung, sharply pressed,
from his imposing arms,

unstoppable legs,
no one wiggled, no one
stuttered, not a hand

went up, not a mouth
opened. No second grader
launched spitballs,

and no first grader giggled,
our breathing muted,
fingers clammy as we

lined up, ascending order—
two-by-two, hand-in-hand.
Wasn't he the tallest black man

any of us had ever seen?
Didn't he have the deepest
voice? We stood there,

trying not to move,
inspected by his unwavering
gaze, more afraid of him

than of our own fathers,
Mr. Richardson more terrifying,
scarier though he couldn't hit us.

Compared to him our fathers
seemed weak, incompetent,
their clothes never as

immaculate, no pinky rings
on their fingers, no gold
cufflinks on their sleeves.

So when I was summoned
to his dim, book-lined office,
I thought I'd surely done evil,

prayed my mother wouldn't
be phoned, hoped somehow
for reprieve. And when

Mr. Richardson called me
by name, I felt fear settle
deep in my queasy tummy.

He handed me a textbook full
of bright pictures—stoplights
turning red, yellow, green,

fire engines racing down tidy
city streets, spotted dogs leaping
in joy. *Read for me*, he ordered,

and I did, voice quavering,
hands shaking, two ungainly braids
sticking out on either side

of my head. Saying nothing,
he took the book back,
sent me back to class

clutching a wooden hall pass.
The next week, I was skipped
to second grade, only a month

in first, still afraid of that
deep voice, still listening
for the thud of Mr. Richardson's

polished shoes, a resonant stomp
that kept us all quiet until he
was far from sight,

the door to his office
clanging closed,
sealed tight.

Appetites

In school, when teachers wanted to bribe us,
they'd haul out bags of potato chips

or pretzels, sacks of bubblegum balls
in every color we prized—an instant party,

immediate relief from fractions, decimals,
the deadening numbers we all hated,

loathing the fact each question
could only take one answer.

Promised junk food if we'd quiet
during grade school math, we'd sit

without fighting or fidgeting,
hands folded on desk tops, mouths shut.

Amazed at how docile we could be
when prodded with candy and snacks,

some teachers celebrated every kid's birthday
by buying chocolate chip cookies

and heavily frosted cupcakes, chocolate icing
melting down their edges, the cake beneath

moist, springy. Some kids lied,
said their birthdays were in October

or November when they were really born
in June or August, just so their hapless teacher

would promise them a party
complete with paper cups full

of fizzy soda, cellophane-wrapped
individual-sized candy bars,

bowls of corn chips and cheese puffs,
those orange concoctions staining

grubby fingers. Every mouthful
tasted better, every chip and every

handful of butter-flavored, artificially-colored
popcorn was better here than at home,

better in a classroom than at Mom's
battered kitchen table. We liked the thrill

of knocking a drink to the floor,
of littering the ground with crumbs

and wadded napkins, sure our teachers
would be too tired to scold us,

so weary from our noise, our prattle,
they'd shoo us from the building,

relieved not to see us again
until the next day, knowing we learned

less and less with each successive grade,
sated by sugar and salt, caramel

and creamy nougat, chewy fudge or
nacho chips—growing up gorged, dumb.

Bullies

O how they loved to tease
the skinny cry-baby girl
I was, with my scrawny arms
and candy-sticky hands,

legs dirty, scabs and sores
picked. Who wouldn't tease someone
whose teeth were rotting from
too much ice cream and soda,

too many trips to the candy counter
day after day after day? Yes,
that shabby girl lisped, stuttered
when nervous, especially when shoved

against the chain-link schoolyard fence,
chattering about what good friends
we all were, how Linda would never
hurt a real friend, how Angie

shared her lunch when soda
exploded in mine. But they'd
have none of that, Linda
pushing my arms and shoulders

back, Angie pummeling my ribsy
belly, pinching and twisting flesh
until I cried, *enough, I'll do
what you want!* They let me

off the fence, smiled smug
little girl smiles, satisfied
I'd do whatever they asked,
whenever they asked.

They told me I'd beat up
a weaker, smaller girl
the next day, that I'd be
there on the playground

at recess to make sure Donya
cried, or they'd beat me
again, and worse, they'd stop
letting me hang around,

revoking that permission.
So I grabbed her, socked her down,
used all my nine-year-old might
to make sure she cried,

thin tears trickling down
her cheeks. *You can't even
cry right,* I sneered, Angie
and Linda cheering approval

at this, laughing hard.
And I wasn't sorry, not glad
when Angie and Linda finally said,
let her up, stop; no, I wanted

to feel Donya's chest heave
just a few minutes more,
hear her sobs and know that I
caused them, nobody but me.

Sleepaway Camp

No counselor could convince me
—scared, shivering girl—
to dive off that splintering dock
and into the lake's torpid waters,

blue-gray suds that didn't subside.
No one, not even Frank, the brown-eyed,
proud-muscled boy who led everyone
in nighttime sing-a-longs, his voice louder

and stronger than anyone's. Not even Mary
with her wheatstraw hair and gentle
voice, her long limbs, nimble fingers
that could brush tears away faster

than any other female counselor's,
those women of seventeen, eighteen.
I stood there, teeth clattering,
one strap of my baggy bathing suit

perpetually falling from my shoulder,
knobby knees knocking together
so loudly I thought everyone
could surely hear their clamor,

everyone ready to laugh and point
at the black girl too scared
to jump in the shallow waters.
The black boys didn't act this way—

they charged into the water unafraid,
wearing only underwear, whooping,
hollering, kicking and diving.
But this black girl, they thought,

doesn't she know what we've done
for her?—two whole weeks of summer fun,
wholesome air, real swimming instead
of prancing in front of a filthy hydrant.

But I didn't care if I was
a charity case, didn't care
that the camp director came over,
her pleated khakis crisp,

silver whistle dangling
from a thin lanyard around
her neck—I wasn't going to go
anywhere near water

because my mother had spent hours
straightening my thick hair, tugging
it with a fiery hot comb so I'd be
presentable at camp, not the object

of anyone's pity. She'd pulled
and combed until my scalp was sore,
my hair straight enough for me to handle
as long as my head never got wet,

no sweating, no dunking, no lake.
So when the camp director said,
what's the matter, sweetie,
are you scared, I told her

my mama said I couldn't swim,
said it wasn't good for me,
made me sick, and could I go home
now, back where there were

no lakes to fall into?
The camp director laughed,
patted my bony shoulder, said,
you won't want to go home

in a few days—her blue eyes merry,
voice musical. She smiled,
you'll love it, you'll see,
but I never did see, never let

water come anywhere near my head,
not even in the showers,
hearing Mama's warnings
all the while: *don't you*

dare come back home
with no nappy head I can't
comb, stay out of that
damn water, you hear?

Who You Calling Ugly?
or When Black Ceased to be Beautiful

Liver-lips, nappy head,
you so ugly no one wants
to be seen with you,
much less talk to you
on these streets.
You so damn dark
no one can see you,
lights off or on!
Better get some
skin-tone cream,
lighten up that face,
those ashy elbows,
those stick legs.
I know you think thin
is in, but girlfriend,
you so damn skinny
that if you turned
to one side, you'd
disappear, narrow
as cracks on pavement.
You, my friend,
have no reason to strut
or parade: you have no butt,
no booty to swing;
your hair so short
no straightening comb
or curling iron
can help you, no relaxer,
curly perm or jar
of miracle hair-grow pomade

will work. Hard to tell
if you are a girl,
if that's what you are
with your torn-up sneakers,
hand-me-down t-shirts.
You give your mama
a bad name dressing like that:
where are your gold chains,
earrings, rings, bracelets,
your nail polish, rouge,
where are your pantyhose?
Put something on those legs,
those bare feet, cover them
so I can't see how you let
them get even darker in summer.

For once,
show some pride.
Put on a dress, put some grease
in those naps, some new clothes
that don't look like something
your father threw out years ago,
shoes like rowboats. Maybe if
you start to look like a woman,
I'll take you out, show you off
like I just bought you new
from the store. It couldn't hurt
to look like you desire men,
like you want to be wanted.

It couldn't hurt to straighten
what little hair you have,
to put a bra on that tiny chest.
And keep your mouth closed
so no one can see how wide
your lips are, how big
the gap between your
two crazy crooked teeth.

II

Mrs. Gaither

That little brown bird of a woman
would make us sing anything—
corny tunes like "Zing! Went the Strings
of My Heart" or showstoppers like

the theme from *Oklahoma!*, though
none of us would probably ever see
winds sweeping down those plains.
Calling each group up front—

the high screeching sopranos first,
then the wobbly mezzo sopranos,
and finally, the overwhelming altos,
she'd pound her stubby fingers

on the worn yellowed keys of
our classroom piano, a cranky upright
with a peeling brown veneer,
yelling more *tone, more tone!*

in her quick, clipped speech,
yelling *I can't hear you, altos!*
to the deepest voices in the room.
Busy in her plaid pleated skirts,

bow-tied blouses, she flitted
around the room in clunky high heels,
bringing us back together
after rehearsing each part

separately, exhorting us
unison, children, unison!
trying to blend our motley voices
into some semblance of music,

praying to hear something
faintly tuneful, something
recognizable to all those parents
who came to every holiday concert,

melodies to soothe those mothers
and fathers with their goofy smiles,
flash cameras. She even taught us
a Hanukkah song—*come see the candles burning,*

see them burning so brightly—told us
the story of the deeds of the brave
Maccabees, smiling at Gina Gordon,
the only Jewish girl in class.

I longed to be her favorite,
but could never stay in range,
my mezzo soprano lazily slipping
to the deeper alto part, my ear

unable to hear what resided between
high and low, my voice wavering
as I fell behind trying to recall
what I'd learned minutes earlier,

so that Mrs. Gaither had to take me
aside, pound out the right notes
all over again so I could hear,
my knees quaking when she called

me, disappointment on her face
as she whispered *you just don't
listen, do you?*, her patience spent
on me, on all the untalented

girls like me whose parents
she smiled for when those
holiday concerts rolled around.
Those nights, when we

took the stage in our
crisp white blouses,
our ironed pants and skirts,
Mrs. Gaither would grin

and bear our sounds, wishing,
perhaps for a real chorus
instead of her gawky singers,
some too timid to sing

with force, some too skittish
to keep still on the risers,
some not smart enough
to remember their parts

in the harmony,
their small shares
of memorized music,
practiced melodies.

What Friends Are For

What were the three of us doing
roaming Macy's lower level,
happy among high-priced furniture
our parents couldn't afford,

didn't buy? Lured by this glimpse
of how our futures could be,
April, Lizette, and I ambled
through that store for hours,

and no adult bothered us,
no security guard held us back,
no store employee questioned
why we weren't in school

but were here instead,
stepping cautiously among
burnished drop-leaf oak tables,
ornate armchairs and loveseats

done in scrollwork and velvet,
plush sofas we'd sit on for
only a minute, stroking the fabric,
loving the chaste weave of new cloth.

We studied everything we saw—
chaise lounges chic in black
leather, recliners so enticing
we stretched out regally

in them, sneakers in the air,
king and queen-sized beds
free of stains and spills,
coils intact, covers pristine.

We told each other that afternoon
we'd all live together one day
in a house where all the furniture
looked as new and clean as this,

that we'd have floors and rooms
to fill with cabinets and cedar
chests, curtains and chandeliers,
that we'd set exquisite tables

of long-stemmed elegant glasses
and lustrous silverware,
eating off flawless white china,
not spilling one drop on tablecloths

of finest snowy linen. We'd have
fabulous jobs, of course, leaving
our house every morning in heels,
tailored suits, doing glamorous work

for fantastic money, though we weren't sure
just what such a job would entail.
Two black girls, one Puerto Rican,
we vowed to be grown together,

to live lives of such ease and grace
no one would dare call us ugly,
tease us about our hair or clothes.
We each arrived home long after

school was done, our mothers demanding
to know where we had been as they stood
in doorways of our ordinary houses
full of worn sofas, trampled cushions,

scratched and scraped chairs
that didn't match, furniture too old
for the house we dreamed of,
the home our mothers could never own.

School Lunches

We did anything to avoid them,
including going hungry
from 7:30 in the morning
to 3:30 in the afternoon,

including sneaking off-campus
to the Italian delis and pizza shops
lining Bedford Park Boulevard.
Insistent odors of too many meals,

ripe scents of tuna casseroles
and sloppy Joes, the sight
of too many gray meat patties
covered with the thinnest slice

of plasticized cheese was
too much for us, so much so
that we risked life, limbs,
and threats of detention

to cross four lanes of traffic
running to the closest candy store.
Sure, we knew about the four
food groups, knew what our

growing bodies needed,
but still somehow found it hard
to lift our plastic forks
for another bite of chili mac,

of turkey croquettes or chicken a la king,
every dish the same solid sluggish
consistency, hardly mobile
on our stiff cardboard platters.

Smart students planned
ahead, made lunches at home,
but most of us, lazy,
forgetful, didn't

pack a paper bag full
of safe sandwiches
and blemish-free fruit.
Some would starve,

some might steal,
but most of us would queue up
on the cashier's line again,
praying for something better

than fried fish fillets
toughened as rubber,
chicken patties breaded
in a cheerless orange coating,

hot dogs popping loose
from their pink casings,
by-products inside
rigid as ragged leather.

What We Once Wore

Please, put that photo album away—
I don't want to remember
that I once wore neon-green
short-shorts, tube socks past

my knees, and t-shirts
with contrasting piping
on plunging scoop necks.
I thought I looked cute

in thick-soled, plush suede sneakers,
also green, with laces so yellow
it hurts, it actually hurts,
to remember them. Once I

favored tube tops—ribbed garments
so tight, so shot through with elastic
they left marks on my flat chest,
or so loose they constantly slipped

down, flimsy fabric around my navel.
Floral print halter tops
with matching maxi-skirts, chunky
high-heeled sandals, cork-bottomed—

I wore them all, in patterns
and colors to scary to confess.
But don't laugh—I know what's
at the back of your closets:

forest green knickers you wore
one Saint Patrick's Day
for a puny, festive look,
"urban cowboy" shirts you thought

both you and John Travolta
looked good in, polyester tank tops
that stretched as your midriff grew
incredible, inevitable. And ladies,

I know you have some horrors
back there too: jumpsuits
with too many zippers
to all stay closed at once,

bathing suits with reflector panels,
torn t-shirts left over from
your miscalculated plunge into
the aerobics craze. It pains you too

to think of how long your collars once were,
how shiny your acrylics, how you once
dressed in plaids so busy they brought
on vertigo, stripes too broad to ignore.

Explaining Sex to the Seventh Grade

No teacher wanted that task:
explain human reproduction
in two weeks, the only time
the state allotted to detail
those secret workings to teenagers
who couldn't sit still, couldn't
be alone, groping each other
during breaks between classes,
slowing hallway traffic for kisses
that never seemed to stop until
someone stopped them, until
a teacher pulled the boy and girl
apart, told them to go to class,
knowing the next period
the same couple would be at it
again, kissing so fervently
everyone would watch, his arms
tight around her skinny waist,
her lips clumsy on his neck.
But unlucky Mr. Harris
taught Hygiene as well as gym,
had the honor of showing us films
on good manners, good nutrition,
gleefully telling us about the importance
of calcium for strong bones,
warning about the horrors
of rickets, scurvy, pellagra.
But on pages 253 to 258
lurked all he didn't want to talk
about: sperm swimming by millions
into an anonymous vagina,
wriggling their way through

a fluted, narrow cervix
into the womb and on to
the Fallopian tubes to find the egg
that could start a life, make a baby
like the babies a few girls left school
to have, his lecture too late for them.
We acted as if we'd heard it all before,
and we had, except we'd whispered
dirty words instead of proper ones,
drawn crude pictures of bulging
breasts and crotches on our desks,
in our texts, rude approximations
of what Mr. Harris now described,
color rushing bright to his normally
pale cheeks, his slight stammer
worsening each time he said *penis*
or *vagina*, every time he pointed
to the text's curt illustrations
of male and female anatomies.
His shirt clung damp to his chest,
inky sweat rings grew wide
on his sky-blue t-shirt,
his blond hair matted as if
he were coaching the boys'
basketball team, running wind sprints
down and up the court.
We girls rolled our eyes,
stifled laughs, trying not to embarrass
the one teacher whose length and size
we'd wondered about, every other teacher
too old for sex in our opinion,
too old, too ugly. So Ralphie

spoke up first, wanted to know
what if felt like the first time
Mr. Harris did it, asking
was she stacked?, Ralphie's palms open
as if he were holding big ones,
teasing, *How long did it take,*
Mr. Harris, did ya get off?
Harris said nothing, too stunned
for anger, too shamed to threaten
to kick Ralphie out of class
like he threatened almost every class,
too sweaty and nervous to say anything
except *class dismissed*, though
we had ten minutes left,
time enough for him to explain it
again, to tell us what we thought
we knew all about, define it again
until we saw no pleasure in it,
only the frigid clarity
of illustrations and diagrams,
pictures no one could possibly
get off on, not even Ralphie,
his hands shifting under his desk,
a dreamy smile on his lips.

Fourteen

Eyebrows plucked, face scoured,
skin taut from astringents,
acne creams, I'm punished by

blemishes erupting across
my broad sweaty forehead.
Mother pulls my hands off,

scolds *don't touch, they'll*
only grow worse, as if
they could grow worse,

already peering beneath bangs.
Each spot looms large,
prominent on nose, cheeks,

and I'm sure no boy will
talk to me when I look
this way, complexion out

of control, body skinny,
nowhere near curvaceous,
no breasts to compensate

for the state of my skin.
I try to keep my face
averted, holding my head

at some weird angle,
as if a certain tilt
could keep these flaws

from light, keep
everyone from staring
at a face I think hideous,

absurdly ducking behind
textbooks and paperbacks,
walking the halls at school

with eyes down, head down,
never seeing all those
other teenaged faces

as bothered and blistered
as mine, just as shamed,
trying just as hard not

to be noticed, not to be
seen slinking home from
class, hoping for a cure

in the latest lotions,
newest, harshest chemicals
we could splash on or rinse off,

going home to scour our faces
again, trying to scrub away
every imperfect, impertinent blot.

Music Appreciation

Stalking the room like a mad conductor,
Mr. Lombardi assailed our ignorance,
defiled our love of popular music
when we could have been listening
to Bach's glorious violin concertos,
full of intricate baroque embellishments,
or the crashing fervor of the "1812 Overture,"
which he played at stentorian volume
so our seats shook, ears throbbed,
or the American splendor of Aaron Copland,
his "Appalachian Spring" only marginally appealing
to a class of surly teens from the Bronx,
kids whose greatest musical controversy
pitted white-boy rock against emerging
street rap: Jethro Tull versus Grandmaster Flash,
Rush versus Run D.M.C. In washed-out
corduroys, worn boots, and shirts we speculated
he'd bought before we were born,
Lombardi paced up and down, pivoting
to scrawl indecipherable notes on the board,
his hair wild but thinning, growing more disheveled
each time he ran his fingers through it,
each time he shook his head when someone
gave the wrong answer regarding the reason
for Gregorian chants, music we all found
maddening in its monotony, its utter calm.
He'd sit on the teacher's desk instead of
behind it, pounding his heels against it
to get our attention, pissed off when we
booed "The Rite of Spring," hating

the jarring sounds we couldn't identify,
angering him even more when we called
it noise, taunting him so he'd kick the desk.
Its wood finally gave in, desk
slumping to the floor with an ugly thud
that wouldn't have been out of place
in Stravinsky's discordant masterpiece.
That semester, Lombardi played us
the opening notes to Beethoven's Fifth
for weeks on end, claiming that was where
it all began, where every musician
was stealing from, everything after
a cheat, a scam on Beethoven's genius,
a mind we couldn't possibly comprehend,
our ears sullied by silly radio pap,
our heads too vacant to recognize
the soaring beauty of Handel's *Messiah*,
passionate heartache of *Porgy and Bess*,
Gershwin too rarefied for kids who'd
mix up *crescendo* and *decrescendo*,
legato with *glissando*, *forte* with *pianissimo*.
Maybe we'd have been better off
in Mr. Morgenstern's Musical Performance class,
trying to exact sound from school-owned
clarinets and flutes, maybe we would have
learned more trying to make our own music.
But we would have missed the fury
of Lombardi, one skinny, wiry flame of a man
determined to save us from the primitive
percussion of rock and rap, the beat
we swore we couldn't live without.

Anti-Prom

Who needs to be prom queen
when the whole city beckons,
so much more glamorous at night
when everything glistens—

neon of club marquees,
signs of all-night diners?
I needed no corsage
pinned to my dress

or forced on my wrist,
needed no stretch limo,
because the streets and subways
would do, so much more alive,

so winningly perverse.
All I needed was a slinky dress,
slits up its sides,
studded belt, strapless shoes.

Able to subsist on meager notions
of romance, all I wanted to do
was dance with someone not
in high school, not in polyester.

Bold, I didn't even need ID—
what club wouldn't want
my girlfriends and me to jazz
up the place, add class beyond belief.

But somehow the management
of every club in downtown Manhattan
knew every high school kid was coming
in tonight from the other four

boroughs, longing to get in,
to dance, to drink what they could
on limited funds, and no bouncer
wanted his club overrun with

jittery underage boys and girls
up late past bedtime. So they
turned us away in groups,
us girls shivering as cold wind

picked up our skirts or dresses,
our legs freezing in fishnet.
They let us in before, I grumbled,
and someone grumbled back,

that wasn't prom night.
We were all too obvious
in our miniskirts and lipgloss,
borrowed high heels beginning

to chafe our feet. Every club
turned us away, no matter
how cute we looked when we tried
to cajole the doormen, no matter

how many of us begged *please,*
please, complete with desperate
attempts at flirty talk,
body language.

We ended up in a filthy dive
called The Dive, a hole too crass
for its minuscule cover charge.
A punk band thrashed away,

too tired, terrible and loud
to get a gig any place better,
its members probably thrilled
to play in New York, even if

that meant this rusty club
where no one danced, laughed,
applauded. Rubbing my feet,
wincing over each caustic riff

the cadaverous lead guitarist
scratched out, I wanted no more
to do with prom night,
the whole concept condemned.

I took the subway home alone,
purse clutched tight in one hand,
shoes gripped in the other,
cursing everyone who'd ever

had a date, who'd lined up two
by two for the actual prom,
those couples now safely asleep
in the backs of cushy limos.

Supermercado

The tv ads thunder "tops en el Bronx!"
so my father and I make a pact,
set out in pursuit of fruit
to a warehouse turned supermarket
with sawdust on the floors and crates
cracked open in the aisles,
more abundance here than in scanty
neighborhood stores, so much
to pick through, mull over:
peaches so ripe in their blushing
fuzzy skins we are tempted
to munch them right there,
juice seeping down our chins
like water seeping into earth.
Here we are brown people unashamed
to love watermelon, stereotypes giving way
when we see that red-pink flesh
that we know is juicier than any kiss,
welcoming even the unobtrusive seeds
that will slip subtly from our mouths.
My father hands me three plastic bags,
pushes me toward mounds
of lemons, limes, tangerines,
chiding me to find the best ones,
unblemished, almost ready,
globes of yellow and orange,
each one a world I admire,
feeling its nubby skin just moments
before I tuck it in the right bag.

Why have mere grapes when
mangoes beckon, when we can taste
the extravagance beneath
their green-going-yellow-going-red skins,
when we can imagine mango pulp—
sweet and tart and light on our tongues.
Apples are too ordinary for us
when here we can buy huge coconuts
we'll later crack open, sip cool
sugary water from, when we can indulge
in pineapple, kiwi, pomegranate,
fruit congregating in our basket,
then in the car, bounty
in our rusty Chevy, in all
the not-so-sleek cars of our city
carrying away this fruit,
plump flesh enfolding pits,
tang singing beneath rinds.

College Tour

The naked woman on screen
bucks and heaves in pleasure,
thrusting her hips forward,
then back, slipping her vibrator

over what I can hardly watch,
her sweaty skin flushing red,
my cheeks flushing hot in shame.
It's prospective weekend, and I'm

17, stunned by sex on campus,
by this human sexuality lecture
complete with overhead presentations
and discussion groups after;

coed, of course, so I hide
in the corner, in the back
of the room, so no one can ask me
if I think vibrators are essential

for effective masturbation.
No one told me college would be
anything like this: that I'd eat
in a basement co-op

where I'd mistake eggs benedict
for soup, drinking the rich sauce
down before the servers could bring
the eggs from the kitchen,

the sauce making me so ill
that I felt green, had to dash
to the bathroom. That I'd hear
black students complain bitterly

about whites and their racism,
so much so that they had
their own dorm, their own
literary magazine and newspaper,

even their own cafeteria
where whites couldn't eat,
even if they wanted to,
even if they asked.

My black hosts laugh
when I tell them I'd eaten
at the underground co-op,
rolling their eyes, giving

each other knowing looks.
But I don't know who
to hate yet, who the targets are
among the stately stone buildings,

the landscaped shrubs and trees,
among the sweatshirts and tie-dye,
the ripped jeans my mother
would have torn up for rags.

No one could have known
that I'd stammer my way
through an interview
in an English professor's office—

stuttering as I look at all
his books, scattered papers,
his sparse gray hair uncombed,
his glasses slipping off,

clattering to the floor
and onto the ground as he
gives me book after book,
enticing me with words,

telling me I could be
the next Gwendolyn Brooks
as long as I studied with him,
in his classes, that he knew

what to do with my promise,
my potential. Then I feel his hand
—slight, cold, trembling—
on my forearm, shoulder, my cheek.

It stays there until I pull
away, mystified by a touch so nervous
yet so gentle I can pretend
that he hadn't touched me at all.

Numbers

My father taught me to measure
the worth of any good thing
by the number of black people
involved. Without sufficient numbers,

he wouldn't root for a team,
wouldn't eat in a restaurant,
wouldn't turn on his television
to watch a local newscast

that didn't have a black anchor.
He wanted black people
to appear on *Masterpiece Theatre*
—he'd lived in England so he knew

black people lived there—
wanted us on *Evening at Pops*
and *Live from Wolf Trap,*
the orchestra's black musicians

conveniently placed up front
for his recognition, wanted
every diva who performed at the Met
to be brown, proud, beautiful—

an endless string of Jessye Normans
and Leontyne Prices. He'd rage
at commercials, at *The Brady Bunch,*
at soap operas, Broadway musicals,

at any bit of American culture
tossed before us as entertainment
that dared not have a black cast member.
So I grew up rooting against the then

all-white Mets, the Boston Red Sox,
(Jim Rice their only saving grace),
the Celtics, hell, the whole city of Boston,
the obscene snowy landscape of New England.

So he probably thought he'd failed
to instill his wisest lesson
when we drove to that college
in middle-of-nowhere Ohio

with its green clapboard shutters
on its white colonial cottages,
its manicured hedges
and windowboxes of tulips.

Resolute, he helped me hoist boxes
to my narrow, undecorated room,
watched glumly as Mom unpacked
suitcases, as my sister folded clothes.

Suspicious, he finally asked,
where are all the black people,
but I could show him only three faces
in the freshman picture book,

including my own photo booth snapshot.
He thought I was crazy to live
so close to them, the white people
who'd conspired so long against him,

the numbers on that campus
far too low for him, my scholarship
bleaching me, making me
less black, less daughter.

Cammie Cuts My Hair

for Cammie McGovern

Tentative at first, she snips off millimeters,
not sure how to cut hair
that's half kinky, half-straight,
or rather, half-natural, half-relaxed—
"relaxed" the odd beauty school word
for black hair stricken by chemicals.
Nothing in R.A. training prepared her
to cut my hair, hair of the only
black girl in that dormitory,
in that freshman class.
Snipping deeper and deeper,
she cuts off spiky split ends
until my true curl surfaces,
a soft kink rare on this campus
of bottle blondes, freckled redheads,
brunettes fluent in curling iron.
How I've envied them,
believing white girls prettier
than black, envying hair
not tortured by lye.
But now, as Cammie cuts,
we're both amazed at the texture emerging
beneath her hands: strong, soft, springy,
alive to itself, a deeper color, truer black.
How strange that it's a white woman
who gives me back my hair,
saying, *look, do you like it,*

as dormitory bathroom light
sifts down upon us both,
and I touch the tender skin
where scalp meets nape
as if for the first time.

Fellowship

Young voices in the service of the Lord
are here to sing for my mother,
radiant teens with tambourines
who sing and pray to ease her pain,
heal the sickness that's taken
over her body, cancer that's
whittled her thin, made her shaky,
cautious, unable to lift
her limbs from bed. They sing
in English, in Spanish,
eager voices of praise
my father cruelly mimics,
resenting "Jesus-lovers" in his house,
fuming in front of his television.
They sing "What A Friend We Have
In Jesus," testifying to His love
with eyes closed—Miguel and Ana
shaking their tambourines so that
shimmering sound surrounds my mother,
Antonio fingering his guitar,
strumming songs I hear as I stand
in the hallway, door open just enough
for me to see how they pray,
how they lay their hands on her,
calling the disease out,
pulling it out like a poison,
willing it out with faith.
They touch her in ways
I'm afraid to, tell her Jesus won't
let her down, won't abandon her,

that soon sweet heaven will embrace her,
make nil this earthly pain.
O how they pray: voices rising, falling,
whispering *Jesus, Jesus,*
bless this woman, Lord,
bless her and know her and love her
as she knows and loves your Word,
voices doubling, tripling
from the five of them
in her room, by her side.
I'm too afraid to go in,
to stand among them so that
the Lord can touch me too,
can know what's in my heart.
But all that's in my heart
is the fear my mother will die,
the knowledge that these faces—
serene, beaming with Jesus' love—
won't be here when she does.

III

In the Spirit: On Seeing the Sounds of Blackness Perform, Riverfront Park

My body sways in a kind of joy
I never thought I'd know, feet
unmindful of where they land,
moving to please themselves,
my arms above my head
wanting to embrace this music,
to pull these resonant voices
into my own body, so I'd always
hear such profound basses,
triumphant sopranos,
this blending and melding
of low and high tones
turning each song into an ocean
that surges above me, thrilling
with wave after celebratory wave.
I thought I was immune to gospel,
to hymns and spirituals,
but these knowing faces,
these swelling vocals,
I cannot resist them, cannot stop
my body from swaying along
when the soloist steps forth
to give us her richest notes,
her voice ascending and ascending
into realms I never dared
believe in, places I glimpse
if only for this moment,

this confluence of organ, tambourine
and these many mighty voices,
this choir undaunted by the pain
in the music of a people:
slave songs, work chants,
passionate psalms of praise
that soothe and sustain,
giving solace to even a doubter
like me, a woman who never before
danced in public, a woman who is now
dancing with every ounce of spirit
she has—snapping fingers,
clapping hands, moving hips
to the music of this multitude,
the varied voices buoying
her up, making her know God.

"Imitation of Life"

So what if I've seen it
a half-dozen times,
when that movie crops up
in mid-afternoon or the middle

of the night, I'm drawn to the tv
as if I have nothing better to do,
as if my life depends on seeing
two daughters betray their mothers,

then live to regret it.
And I'm not talking about
the refined black and white original
with Claudette Colbert and Louise Beavers,

the version where the daughter
who looks white but is black
is actually played by an actress
who looked white but was black.

Her name? Fredi Washington,
and she was lovely enough
to be a star, but Hollywood
had no clue what to do with

a black actress whose light skin
would make her look silly
in a maid's uniform. No, the version
that hooks me every time

is the gaudy Technicolor remake,
a film stopped in its tracks
whenever Madame Lana Turner
appears on screen, her blond coiffure

fancy whether her character's rich
or poor, hourglass figure emphasized
even when she's supposed to be
a dowdy widow with no funds,

a stage actress wannabe.
In this version, like the first,
a black woman and a white woman
move in together to raise

their daughters, fend off poverty.
But all Lana cares about
is becoming a star, so her black friend
really raises both girls—

who grow up to be Sandra Dee
and an actress who looks like Natalie Wood,
but isn't, a white woman playing
at being a black girl

who looks white. It's she
who truly fascinates—her
performance pouty, impetuous,
not merely tragic like Fredi Washington's,

but so blatant you forget Lana's
in the movie, so histrionic
I laugh out loud whenever this
Natalie Wood look-alike screams

she wants to be *white, white, white*
because that's exactly what she is!
I can't resist the scene where she's
run away from home, joined

a chorus line, finally able to pass as white,
dancing at a seedy club for dollars a week.
So thrilled is she not to be called
Sarah Jane—a colored girl's name if ever

there was one—that she rejects her mother,
her long-suffering, dark-skinned mother,
lets her fellow chorus girls think
she was raised by a mammy, a Negro cook.

I can't help roaring with abrupt laughter
at the end when the Natalie Wood look-alike
returns, stumbling back home, knowing somehow
her mother was dead, stung by her daughter's

spite. The funeral's fantastic, attended
by every black Central Casting could find,
complete with gospel solo by Mahalia Jackson
herself. When Sarah Jane comes running in

to sprawl across her poor dead mother's
casket, clawing at the coffin lid, crying
copious tears, sputtering that she really
did love her mother, I'm nearly convulsed

by these hilarious Hollywood ironies,
such delicious contradictions. I'm always
left wondering whose life this movie
is an imitation of, whose version

of black and white, mother and daughter.
Certainly not mine or yours, not anyone's
with sense enough to know tearjerker
movies are like cotton candy—

something that looks like
nourishment but isn't,
concoctions too cloying
to ever be good for you.

Shake Your Body

for Michael Jackson

This is the Michael
I want to remember:
full lips, Afro large
as life, lithe body
slim but not dangerous,
mouth imploring us
to dance, shout, shake
our bodies down to
the ground, his face
his own, untouched
by surgery. This Michael's
no freak show, his dancing
not reduced to crotch grabs
and pyrotechnics, skin
not powdered beyond
recognition to a zone
neither black nor white,
but phantom–like, pallid
as talc. This Michael
still glittered, still shone,
his nose broad across
his face, hair untouched
by chemicals that would
slick his Afro to a dead
sheen, greasy under
stage lights. This Michael
was on his way to being
a man, a black man,

someone whose albums
I wouldn't hide, whose
voice wouldn't turn into
mere vocal tics, tricks,
a parody of itself,
a joke we're all aware of
except for Michael himself—
who's left behind our
ghettos, our streets,
left behind Detroit
and Newark, Little Rock
and Gary. The Michael
I want to remember
blamed "it" on the boogie—
"it" the energy no one
can deny him, "boogie"
that irresistible urge
to dance—the dance
uncomplicated by the
dancer, uncompromised
as the face he used to possess:
broad, brown, African.

The World's Worst Jukebox

plays every song you've ever hated—
maudlin country ballads and stupid novelty hits,
syrupy pop ditties from the Seventies—
tunes so chipper and insistent
you still know the words after twenty years,
can remember how these songs sounded
coming out of your handheld radio,
hiss slithering from the cheap transistor,
static marking spaces between stations.
It's hard to fathom why
someone would put tunes this bad together,
deliberate cruelty, you think,
as you lean over the shimmering machine
in search of one good song
for your shiny quarter.
You can't deal with hearing
that Captain and Tennille gush
that love will keep them together—
but your other choices are no better—
the Swedish schmaltz of Abba's "Dancing Queen,"
the disco version of the theme to *Star Wars*,
Chuck Berry's number one embarrassment,
"My Ding-A-Ling." There's no Beatles or Stones
on this Wurlitzer, just bland British Invasion wimps
Chad and Jeremy, the simpering corn
of David Gates and Bread. No Sly Stone or Prince
and the Revolution either, but "Kung Fu Fighting"
instead, a song whose phony martial arts shouts
thrilled us all when we were eight.

Groups no one's heard of
since their one chart hit
live on in infamy here: the breathy
vocals of Andrea True, former porn star,
the disembodied female chants of Silver Convention,
another Eurodisco product of interchangeable
singers. There are two different versions
of "Muskrat Love," every smarmy hit
by Air Supply, and singles from bands
whose very names are bad omens:
Vanilla Fudge, Pink Lady, the Chipmunks.
You want to grab someone, anyone,
want to collar the bar's manager
for an explanation, demanding the name
of the person who did this, threatening
to storm his house to ask how anyone
could give us a jukebox with no Supremes
or Vandellas, but with the Crystals singing
"He Hit Me and It Felt Like a Kiss,"
a dirge with lyrics so vile
few stations ever played it,
a song no one will punch,
not even on this jukebox.

Goodbye, Chateau West Apartments and Townhomes

Goodbye giant roaches
that scurried and scuttled into nooks,
crannies seemingly far too small
for their shellac-shiny bodies,
impatient antennae. Goodbye

cracks in the ceiling, gaps
in the plaster that gushed water
when it rained, streams pouring
into every bucket and pan,
every wastebasket dragged

into the kitchen to catch the overflow,
the dishwater-gray water that flooded
the kitchen tile until the linoleum peeled,
buckling back from the corners,
wrinkled as an aged hand.

Goodbye shaky toilet
that ran for twenty minutes
after every flush
though we'd all jiggle the handle
to make it stop, damning

that noisy plumbing, its ceaseless gurgle
echoing in our ears like the roar
of some particularly nasty sea
no one ever wanted to visit.
Goodbye chipped bathroom tile,

goodbye shower stall that leaked
runoff into the living room,
dampening the carpet, baseboards,
moisture always creeping underfoot
despite rent paid on time,

despite the maintenance man's
constant efforts, obvious valor.
Goodbye parking spaces strewn
with broken glass, goodbye
potholes in the asphalt

that were never filled properly
after the gas company came on the property,
dug up the pavement, and left, goodbye
stolen mail and lost letters,
goodbye to dumpsters full

of sodden plastic bags
and irretrievably rusted toys,
busted bicycles and leaky
fast food cartons, goodbye
to forty ounce bottles

of Olde English and St. Ides
smashed against the curbs,
malt liquor remnants
of somebody's Saturday night
greeting me on Sunday morning.

Goodbye to it all:
I've turned in the keys,
cut off the gas and cable,
told the electric company
to discontinue their overpriced

service, filled out so many
change-of-address cards that my new address
keeps repeating its hope inside my head:
all will be better on East Grand,
all will be shiny, new—

the key will fit the front door's lock,
the air conditioner won't leak condensation,
and the apartment manager will apologize
for every nick in each door,
every chip in the paint.

Salt

There's a kind of glory in it,
I think, though doctors warn
of havoc it can do set loose
in the body, able to rocket
blood pressure way past danger.

But I crave it nonetheless,
reaching for the fullest shaker,
whitest crystals, pouring it on
everything, anything, adding it
to the pale trickle of flavor

that passes for soup in the
cafeteria, sprinkling it on
the tame grains of rice
and tepid wilting leaves
from the market's salad bar,

not denying its sting
over chicken noodle casserole
or macaroni and cheese,
homey foods too plain to eat
without salt, too boring

to consider without that
familiar burn, that fall of white
raining down on warmed-over leftovers.
How else could anyone eat
dingy washes of boiled broccoli

or formerly frozen carrots faded
beyond recognition, vegetables
far too blanched to think of
without salt's savvy tossed
on top? And when I say I'll cut

down, I'll take the shaker off
the table, there's always butter,
molten and balmy in saltiness,
always cheese, its sharp tang
of sodium intact whether you

grate it, slice it, melt it.
Yes, my thirst is incredible,
lush, wanton, so thick I drink
far too many glasses
of water per day, that fluid

swelling membranes, cavities.
If I could I'd return
to that childhood Jamaica trip:
salty water, bluer than I ever knew
water could be, buoying me up,

slipping past my lips into my mouth,
beloved taste of home in seas
I'd never seen before. Relatives
still say I couldn't get enough,
child who didn't want to leave

the sea, who drank that water
deeply, flooding my mouth with it,
loving its prickle on my tongue,
knowing it belonged far within,
where nothing else could reach.

On Being Told I Don't Speak Like a Black Person

Emphasize the "h," you hignorant ass,
was what my mother was told
when colonial-minded teachers
slapped her open palm with a ruler
in that Jamaican schoolroom.
Trained in England, they tried
to force their pupils to speak
like Eliza Doolittle after
her transformation, fancying themselves
British as Henry Higgins,
despite dark, sun-ripened skin.
Mother never lost her accent,
though, the music of her voice
charming everyone, an infectious lilt
I can imitate, not duplicate.
No one in the States told her
to eliminate the accent,
my high school friends adoring
the way her voice would lift
when she called me to the phone—
A-ll-i-son, it's friend Cathy.
Why don't you sound like her,
they'd ask. I didn't sound
like anyone or anything,
no grating New Yorker nasality,
no fastidious British mannerisms
like the ones my father affected
when he wanted to sell someone
something. And I didn't sound
like a Black American,

college acquaintances observed,
sure they knew what a black person
was supposed to sound like.
Was I supposed to sound lazy,
dropping syllables here and there
not finishing words but
slurring their final letters
so each sentence joined
the next, sliding past the listener?
Were certain words off limits,
too erudite for someone whose skin
came with a natural tan?
I asked them what they meant
and they stuttered, blushed,
said *you know, Black English,*
applying a term from that
semester's text. *Does everyone*
in your family speak alike,
I'd ask, and they'd say *don't*
take this the wrong way,
nothing personal.

Now I realize there's nothing
more personal than speech,
that I don't have to defend
how I speak, how any person,
black, white, chooses to speak.
Let us speak. Let us talk
with the sound of our mothers

and fathers still reverberating
in our minds, wherever our mothers
or fathers come from:
Arkansas, Belize, Alabama,
Brazil, Aruba, Arizona.
Let us simply speak
to one another,
listen and prize the inflections,
never assuming how any person will sound
until his mouth opens, until her
mouth opens, greetings welcome
in any language.

Incommunicado

I've lost my daughter's logic,
that sense that lets me know
exactly where my father is

at any given moment.
I can only speculate now:
he's in the bathroom,

stroking his chin,
hating the gray at his temples,
in his beard, wondering

how his face grew those hollows,
shadows, marks of age
every good-looking man fears.

Or maybe he's in his bedroom,
sorting the change on his dresser,
fingering coins from England and Canada

that were once daily currency,
his Caribbean weekly, faded, folded,
unread, his colognes—heavy scents

in dark bottles—his tie tacks
and cufflinks strewn in a silver
tray, lottery stubs from last night

shredded to pieces he sweeps
into a tidy pile, telling himself
it's all right to keep losing

as long as the loss is confined, controlled.
Maybe he's out in the garden,
working though there's no

turning that growth back,
no pulling or grabbing that can
stop those spiny stems,

recalcitrant roots, weeds
and vines bedded deep. If he's
pruning roses, he's wearing

those old grimy gloves
he'd make me wear, if he's
raking, it's with the same

rusty, toothless rake
I used to trip over, so clumsy
he'd suck his teeth in disgust.

Maybe the garage, though,
maybe he's there, sifting
through remainders of all

his failed enterprises:
phones, file cabinets,
the waterlogged executive desk.

But I like best to think of him
in the kitchen, stirring
some dish I would never eat—

not now, not then, not ever—
shrimp smothered in onions,
pepper sauce, bay leaves,

oily gravy over his rice,
a mess of yams and pigeon peas
boiling over on the range top.

If the food is filling, warm,
maybe he'll eat another plate,
maybe he'll think quietly

of me, daughter who turned her back,
left him behind for places on the map
no one else bothers with.

Maybe he'll think of forgiveness,
how it starts small—with one meal,
one bowl, one satiating, salty mouthful.

Father Meets Satchmo in Heaven

Louie lights up a spliff
generously given to him by Bob Marley,
breathing the sweet aromatic smoke
he's never been able to renounce,

not even here in heaven,
every bite of celestial hash
is better than the finest drug.
It's an earthly habit

Louie's never been able to break,
fingers just needing
to hold and pinch good stuff,
especially after each day's tourists

leave him tired and dejected,
usually old white women
with kooky Minnie Pearl hats
and straw bags, ninnies

who want to know whether
Grace Kelly really was that beautiful,
or how that Streisand girl was
when she sang "Hello Dolly!"

as if Satch cared about those
white stars, then or now,
elated now not to grin
and smile for a bit part

in a movie, glad to never again
play the happy Negro with a horn.
My father, new to heaven's
celebrity hunt, approaches

with caution, having failed to find
some of the folks he'd wanted
to see most: Clyde Barrow, Dillinger,
Pretty Boy Floyd—white men

with panache, criminals he admired
for their good taste in wine, women,
clothes. But those guys weren't Louie,
so my father perches on a stool

like an anxious schoolgirl
eager to hear what Satch's got to say,
hoping to hear that horn live.
Knowing the bliss of that jazz

Father thinks, *Satchmo'll tear up*
this place without white people around.
Satch looks down, slowly, sadly,
then parts his robes to reveal

two shoes in need of polishing,
says to my father, *how much boy,*
and my father turns paler
than any brown angel ever should,

sputtering that he's no shoeshine boy,
not ever for the greatest horn man
who ever lived. Satch collects himself,
his robes, his spliff, and floats off,

muttering about Negroes in heaven,
how they'll never get anywhere,
without a little spit and polish,
a little deference.